New Wings
And Other Poems

Originally written in Tamil by
AR. Arul Selvan

Translated by
Padmaja Narayanan

Edited by
Mohamed
TransCloud Language Services
Chennai

NOTION PRESS

NOTION PRESS

India. Singapore. Malaysia.

This book has been published with all reasonable efforts taken to make the material error-free after the consent of the author. No part of this book shall be used, reproduced in any manner whatsoever without written permission from the author, except in the case of brief quotations embodied in critical articles and reviews.

The Author of this book is solely responsible and liable for its content including but not limited to the views, representations, descriptions, statements, information, opinions and references ["Content"]. The Content of this book shall not constitute or be construed or deemed to reflect the opinion or expression of the Publisher or Editor. Neither the Publisher nor Editor endorse or approve the Content of this book or guarantee the reliability, accuracy or completeness of the Content published herein and do not make any representations or warranties of any kind, express or implied, including but not limited to the implied warranties of merchantability, fitness for a particular purpose. The Publisher and Editor shall not be liable whatsoever for any errors, omissions, whether such errors or omissions result from negligence, accident, or any other cause or claims for loss or damages of any kind, including without limitation, indirect or consequential loss or damage arising out of use, inability to use, or about the reliability, accuracy or sufficiency of the information contained in this book.

Published Year: 2022

© Copyright: AR. Arul Selvan

To Father...
(The person who encouraged me in writing
and now lives in my memories)

Contents

1. TAMIL

Having learned good Tamil

And acquired poetic skill

Sufferings that flowed on

Did not do affected!

2. TAMILIAN

Tamilian is the world's pioneer

He is mirror that reflects human behaviour!

When the world thought only about food

He constantly thought about morality good!

When many know language only to talk

He scripted life grammar in Tamil to take!

He excelled in art and smelt love flower

He admired priceless valor as eyes forever!

He made things in furnace and liked life of toil

He felt that fame is stable in the world of fickle!

Tamilian is the world's pioneer

He is mirror that reflects human behaviour!

As having love with lore, he welcomed others
He lost all merits by some fox minded crowds!

The fallen Tamilian tries tenaciously to get up
How many hardships he abides to regain
set up!

Though woes follow, he finds a companion as treasure
He discerns that is Tritamil which blooms pleasure!

He begins to break barriers with help of mother tongue
He tends to gain fame on earth that conquers sky!

Tamilian is the world's pioneer
He is mirror that reflects human behaviour!

3. WITNESS

Sight of young crescent in the sky

Girth of mount that hugs by clouds

Whispering river that flows

Music from sliding water of falls

Enchanting rise of the sun

Comforting hearts of women

Sea waves that roll singing

Changes of experience in spring

Carpet of fog on the grass

Smile of the toiling poor

Nature is reigning in these all

Our eyes are witness to those all!

4. THE QUEST AND THE SOLUTION

The God exists – real or not?

Do not waste away your time

By arguing about this!

Because –

The world till not reaches

A consensus "That is God!"

Well!

Is the belief of God need or not?

If the belief brings forth goodness

Let it stay!

If there is no benefit by belief

Let it leave!

5. WHAT NEED?

Oh, Bird...!

We sigh looking at you!

We need a vast mind as yours!

To have that,

Do we need wings?

Or relations like yours?

6. RELIGIONS

Our government which

Fights against drugs,

Nurtures a drug legally!

Yes,

That is religion!

The inventions of man

Perturb himself!

The computer

Snatches his works!

The religion

Divides him from others!

Let the religions

Go away from the earth!

And even before that

Let them go out

From man's mind!

7. SEA WAVES

Oh! Waves, the beautiful arts!

You roll tirelessly,

For you know,

Laziness begets problems?

When we see you,

Dancing in the sea arena,

We forget our woes

And we are enlightened!

When you take a tour

To the shoreside,

By forgetfulness,

You leave the shells that

You bring with you!

You return immediately

To search for them!

Do you think
You can retrieve them?

Don't you know that
Mankind has adept
In plunks away things
Those belong to others?

8. THE NIGHTS

Nights are soothe and sweet!
But the deeds of nights are
Puzzling and incomprehensive!

The sky fills with joy
On the advent of night!
It welcomes the night
With the smile flashes
By its star teeth!

Is the sea
A foe to the night?
It shouts throughout
To send it away!

The philosophers,
The learned,
The knights and
The ambitious
Find the night a challenge!

For mostly
They lose their challenges
In the night,
The night is a
Challenge to them!

Anyhow-
As the nights be
Suitable for lust and sleep
They are soothe and sweet!

9. THE MINDS

Minds are –

The abodes of truth!

The basics of the world!

The pivot of human movement!

The spring of desires!

The wonder mines,

That's depth can't be found!

Mind carries many thoughts

Soft and rough and suaveness

Such the colours are many!

Mankind keeps fighting

Silently with the mind!

When both are mingle-

The classes of society will disappear!

The heaven will descend to earth!

10. BALMING CREATURES

Is it fair that

Close of the entrance

Of your heart

When I ventured to

Answer the questions that

You passed by your eyes!

Why did not you realize

The bliss that

My heart felt

When it found the answers

For the questions

Of your eyes?

I hoped

Your thought would

Ripe like mango flower!

But you proved that

It was jasmine!

I wished to

Win the world and

Gift it you!

But alas!

Nowever my presence

In this world

Could be felt only

By the telling of others!

Only the waves,

Mountains and birds

Are balming

The heart wounds

That were made by you!

11. THE DESIRES

Does the machine ply without fuel?
Does the world move without desires?

Poet's desires are in savour
Youth's desires connect with love
Scholar's desires are constructive
Poor's desires are craving always!

Though human life is a short story
Desires of heart is the running story!

Neglect the advice "Renounce the desire!"
Nurture your desires! But
Let the desires be virtue!
Let the mankind get
Elevation through desires!

12. PUZZLES OF LIFE

Thoughts like paper flowers

The colours of dispersing

The holes that make you stumble

The hearts that are never constant!

The feet that know not the path

The songs which know not language

The dreams which rise in the day

The binds that not match the mind!

The emotions in the sense

The ennuiness of the body

The questions that have no answer

The penances that have no gains!

The wants which are not satisfied

The boats which not reach the shore

The births that daily filled with

The deaths that tomorrow await!

13. SCIENCE

Can prevent the thunder?

Can tear the darkness?

Can drive away the illness?

Can fly in the sky?

'Can do.... Can do...."

Said the science!

Invented equipment,

Landed in the moon,

Broke open the atom

And says now-

It will be possible to remove

The word 'Can't'

From the dictionary!

14. POLITICS

Is it not natural that

The knife of wise person

Peels the fruits

And knife of wicked

Steals the life?

The politics

That the property of people

Resembles the knife!

If the honest holds it,

Outcomes many goodness!

When the vile holds it,

It makes disaster

To the giver!

15. WHY DO YOU MOON?

Oh Moon.... Beautiful moon......!

Why do you hide behind the clouds?

Do the eyes of all men swarm

On you with passion?

Oh Moon.... Blooming moon......!

Why do you appear lean in some days?

Do you see the slender waists

Of the ladies who speak fondling words?

Oh Moon.... Luscious moon......!

Why do you spread cold light rays?

Do you wish to induce attraction

In the eyes of lovers speaking fruit words?

Oh Moon.... Bright white moon......!

Why do you travel fast in the sky?

Do you want to give joy and happiness

To the proletariat who work hard in day?

Oh Moon…. Noble moon……!

Why do you disappear at a time of later day?

Do you like to tell the message that

"Every living being will vanish in a day?"

16. WHERE?

Dear ladies...!

Though the world

Abounds many languages

Where did you learn

The art of speaking by eyes?

Though you adorn

With many jewels

Where did you get a smile

That surpasses them all!

17. SHE

Lovely Statue

Artistic eyes

Jackfruit lips

Breast two mountains

Thread like hip

Banyan leave between thighs!

18. LOVE

The attraction

That evolves naturally

In the hearts!

The bondage that

Nothing can bring apart!

One who researches

It's origin and growth

Surely ends up with failure1

It only has the power

To change a stone to fruit!

And a thorn to flower!

It is a big Question-

When the world would approve this?

The list behind

Romeo-Juliet

Saleem-Anar

Ambikapathy-Amaravathy

Still continues till date!

19. THEN YOU...

My dear...

I crave to claim your heart!

But you refuse even to glance!

I pray for your love!

But you don't form even a think

About me in your mind!

I try to change you!

Can't I?

Then I try to forget you!

Can't I that also?

No, I Can! Yes, I can!

Do you know how?

When I marry the death...

Then I can...

20. DEFEAT

Though he is a valiant knight
To control the fierce bulls,
Though he is a talented warrior
To conquer the rude enemies-
Alas!
He met defeat in the fight
With the eyes of a girl!

21. DO YOU KNOW?

My friend...
Hear... I say to you only!

You know how much he loves me!
Still why do I hurt his heart?
Is it out of extend love?
Or out of my femineity?

I ignore his loving words
When he utters them to me!
But I crave for them
After he departed from me!

I don't see him these days?
Why is he so angry with me?
Has he thought that
I am a proud female?

Is he not aware that

All my beauty awaits for him?

My friend...

Does he atleast know that

He alone is my life?

22. I AND SHE

That was pleasant time of fragile breeze floats

I relished the nature with delightful lady!

There was a tree in front of us and

Two parrots were on branch of the tree!

They were speaking merry stories with happy!

"Do you hear the fruit words of parrots?

Did all languages get birth and grow from them?"

She asked with open out wonder eyes!

I said after relish the wonder beauty of her,

"Are the words of parrots equal or match

To the fondle words that you speak?

Does the sweetness surpass when you implore?

There is no exaggeration, absolutely true!"

"You excel in admiration, but no problem!

Please listen the fertility of the mangoes

That ripen on the tree near that parrot!

Star the attraction of lush fruits like that

Spring season has shaped and come" she said!

I replied in sweet Tamil language clearly,

"Attraction of fruits in the world will fail

Before the luscious charmness of your cheeks

That allure the thoughts of everybody!

I tell my thinking; these are not excelled words!"

She laughed ripely that made her cheeks red!

I had sat silently, she convened me near to her,

"Watch the river that flows from there and

The beauty of fishes, jump here and there in it

Where can we get the immeasurable joy
like this!"

Jasmine natured she said with her bloom face!

I told in adolescent Tamil that change stone
as fruit,

"The fishes coming fast in the silver tide water

Definitely learn the art of jump play for long
time

From your broad eyes that have bow eyebrows!

There is no doubt of little bit my dear...!"

She was looking my face awhile and said,
"Whatever I say, you connect that with me!
What imagination is this!" She got up gently!

23. KNOWLEDGE AND KINDNESS

You inlaid in heart like sim in phone
You made melody by various ringtones
Let's speak and spread love stories only
Let's waft and blow word arrows only!

We may chat through the computer
We may go on date in imagination
Let's write letters in the Facebook
Let's gather joys with "Like" entries!

Though science is governing the world
The love is blowing with beauty!
Though engineering wings prosper in land
The calibre affection grows with manner!

24. THE LIPS

The abode of tastes!

The beginning of ecstasy!

Oh lip... Oh lip...!

Are thou and book... The same?

No! No!

The book reveals benefit

Only when it is opened!

But you are an open wonder!

Only the learned can perceive the book!

But even layman

Can enjoy the taste of you!

25. THE TRUTH

That is true

That is true

The whole world is in it!

Yes!

That is femineity!

That is femineity!

The whole earth is in it!

26. THE KISS

That which

Heats the blood,

Cools the mind

The first stage

Of the nighttime war-

The kiss!

27. THE CHILD

The reign of cradle country

That raised out of the

Cot agreement!

The display of relative nation

That bloomed out of the

Night revolution!

28. ADVICE

Human life consists of puzzles!

It has been made with

Ups and Downs!

So,

Grow the good thought in mind

"I am for you, you are for me

And we are for us"

Do live to evoke

Delight in the world!

29. WET CRACKERS

The promise crackers,

Offered by politicians

At the time of election festival

Were found wet,

When they were fired

In the life house!

30. GUARD

Oh people...

At night times,

Why are you lying down

In the sides of the road,

That was formed by you?

Are you guarding it from theft?

31. THE POVERTY

I don't perturb
About the disgrace on me
Made by some countries!
As my reign is going on
With flag in many countries!

I don't worry
If the cities fail
To welcome me!

For
I remain a permanent guest
In all my loving villages!

I roar with laughter
When some people proclaim
That they would build
A doom for me,
Who dare not meet
Even my heir hungry!

I know it clearly

The coming generations

Would chain me up

Because

I am an accused criminal!

32. I KNOW NOT

I still know not
What freedom is!

When here is not a situation
That all can get definitely
Three square meals a day,

When a group of people
Is sleeping with the
Corner roads as bed

I really know not
What freedom is!

When laborers are drained
And the providence is
Made as the reason

When country abounds with courts
That sell justice
To money and power

I really know not
What freedom is!

When make question…
It is said
"All are being-
That is freedom…!

O hell!
I still know not that
What for we need this freedom?

33. INDIA

As agitation is going on
For food here
Revolutions for rights
Don't explode!

The parliament
Convenes here
To pass some bills
And mainly to list out
Those under poverty line
And assets of the rich!

The people who have
Learned to bow
By the advice of Gandhi
Still have not
Straightened up!

34. EDUCATION

Intelligence evolves

By the measure of

Learning one gets!

'If the education is curbed'

The power gang

Calculates and acts!

When money and education

Are bonded

How long can the

Poor and learning

Stay together?

The looting

That takes place

In schools and colleges

Is called 'Donation!'

The college steps

Are still a mirage

For many downtrodden!

A challenge!

Can the forces which

Restrain a poor student

From obtaining good education,

Stop him from the

Stroll in his dreams as

Doctor or Advocate or Engineer?

35. THE LABOURERS

You the people

Who are born to toil

And the ones

Those mold the world!

Have you ever thought

About your rights?

You bring together the threads

To weave a dress!

You coin together the words

To make a book!

Have you ever thought

About your rights?

You curve the wood

And make many goods!

You raise a doom

And attract all!

Have you ever thought

About your rights?

You pave the roads
And drive the vehicles!
You turnout thousands
In the factories!
But have you ever thought
About your rights?

O tiredless workers...
Are the fear mind
And slave disposition
Your possessions?

As the rotation of earth
Is a nature,
Life Beings revolve only
By your doings!

Perceive and lift up!
Unite and noise up
The right voice!
Do think better
And take decisions
Such as the world adores!
Make a full success!

36. ELECTRICITY

We pass

The life wire

By means of effort magnet!

That's an electro magnet!

Confidence-Electricity!

If Electricity interrupts?

37. THE PATH

The country!

What is a country!

Is it a place

In the world map?

Or a part that

The geography explains?

No, no!

A country means people!

And people mean life!

If we prepare a list

In this perspective-

Can we include our country

Into that list?

Alas! We cannot!

For the caste

Divides the human beings,

For the poverty

Lingers in the homes,
For the money
Reigns throughout-
We cannot!

Well!
Can we do in future?

Why not?
If the youth desire
It could be done!

How?
The young should sharper
Their minds with education flame and
Pave a revolutionary path!
Will there be hurdles and losses?
Yes! There will be!

Can we swim
Without getting wet?
Can we reap
Without sheading sweat?

38. YOU CAN

Hey lads... Lion cubs...!
Hey students...unblemished beads...!

Do try to bend the broad sky
That laughs at poor peasants back!

Do try to capture the sea in your palm
That turned salty by tears of labourers!

Do try to change the breeze as storm
To drive away frenzy rich who exploit workers!

Do start at once with fervour in mind
You and only you can accomplish anything!

39. NEW WINGS

Let's contemplate
Oh, let's contemplate deep!

Let all in the world
Do get the needs
Food, clothe and shelter!

Let one and all attain
The education naturally
That breads good thoughts!

Let rise opinion and writing
Voice and deed
Independently everywhere!

Let's contemplate
Oh, let's contemplate deep!

Let men and women
Mingle in love
And enjoy the bliss forever!

Let do pass the mind
In the scenes of nature
And obtain delight every day!

Let there be the
Generosity of help others
Even during the fall!

Let's contemplate
Oh, let's contemplate deep!

Let form the government
That nurtures the house
And save the land!

Let man get simultaneously
Tenderness, courage
And distinct intellect!

Let there be truth

In the heart

To derive the fruit of life!

Let's contemplate

Oh, let's contemplate deep!

40. HE

He treads his steps
With the support of care!
Nevertheless, jumps over
Lot of hurdles
Between each step!

You may think that
He is joyful!
But you never know
How many hurts are
Still raw in his heart!

His spirit
Carries high ambitions!
Are they only dreams?
Or those that would be
Realized tomorrow?

He accepts mirth silently!

He forgets woes by verses!

He paves the path

For propriety in life! And

He succumbs only to love!

About the Author

AR. Arul Selvan was born on 1961. He retired from India Post Department and resides with family in Chennai. He has been writing in Tamil more than 30 years. His writings were published in magazines, broadcasted through Radio and telecasted by Television. Books with collection of his Poems, Short stories, Articles and Plays have also been published.

Email: writerararulselvan@gmail.com

www.ingramcontent.com/pod-product-compliance
Lightning Source LLC
Chambersburg PA
CBHW040109150726
48005CB00013B/1632